I love reading

Emergency Vehicles

by Monica Hughes

Editorial consultant: Mitch Cronick

CONTENTS

Words in **bold** are explained in the glossary.

Ambulance

An ambulance goes to help people who are hurt or ill.

Blue lights flash.

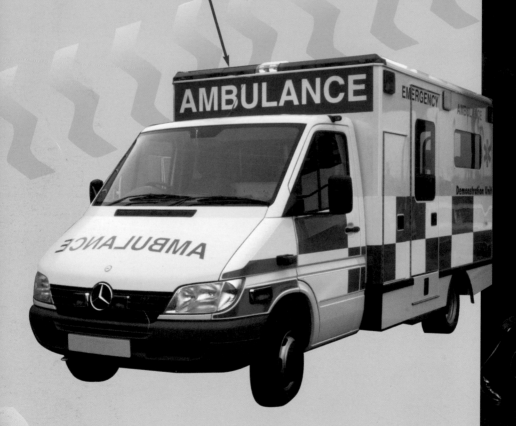

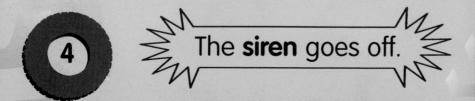

The **siren** goes off.

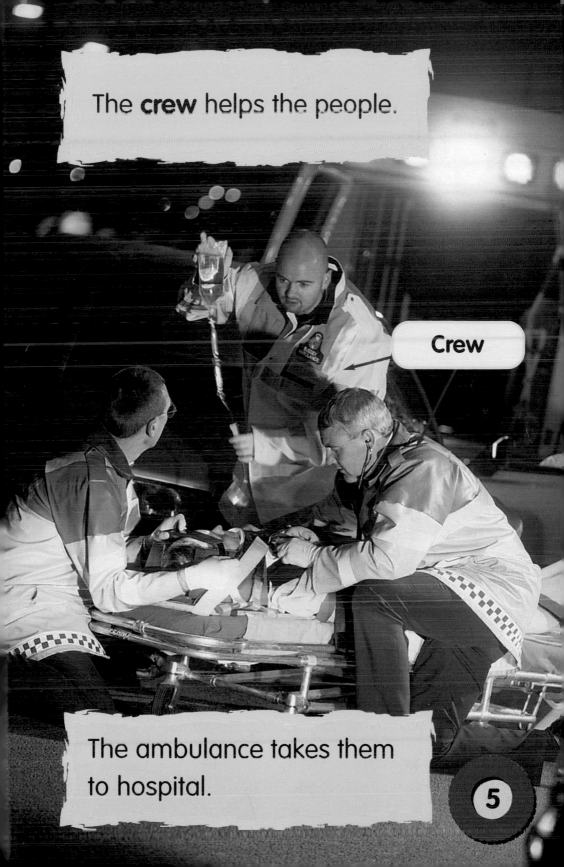

The **crew** helps the people.

Crew

The ambulance takes them to hospital.

Police

There is an accident.

The police go to help.

The police have fast cars.

Flashing lights

The police have fast
motorbikes, too.

The cars have a siren
and flashing lights.

OLICE

W827 AKP

Fire engines

There is a fire.

The fire engine goes to help.

The blue lights flash.

Some fire engines have long ladders.

Ladders

The ladders lift the firefighters up high.

Fighting fires

The fire engine has long hoses.

Hoses

The firefighters spray water on the fire.

The water puts out the fire.

Airport fire

There is a fire at the airport.

The Striker goes to help.

The Striker is a giant fire engine.

It sprays **foam** on the fire.

The foam puts the fire out.

Forest fire

There is a fire in a forest.

An airtanker drops **powder** on the fire.

The powder puts out the fire.

15

Fireboat

The fireboat sprays water on a fire at sea or on a river.

It gets the water from the sea or the river.

LOS ANGELES FIRE DEPARTMENT

DANGER PROPELLERS

17

Snow plough

This road is blocked by snow.

Cars cannot get through.

The snow plough comes to the rescue.

It pushes the snow away.

19

Helicopters

Helicopters can help people who are ill or who are in danger.

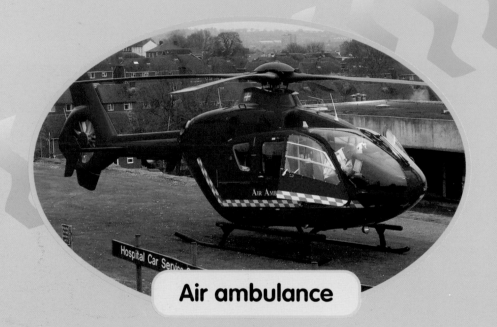

Air ambulance

The air ambulance takes people to hospital.

This helicopter rescues people at sea.

The crew pull people up on a rope.

Glossary

crew

The people who make up a rescue team.

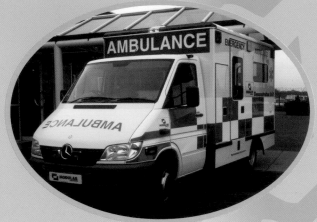

foam

Chemicals in the form of thick bubbles.

powder
Chemicals in the form of tiny soft grains.

siren
A loud wailing sound used as an alarm.

Index

Copyright © ticktock Entertainment Ltd 2008
First published in Great Britain in 2008 by ticktock Media Ltd.,
Unit 2, Orchard Business Centre, North Farm Road, Tunbridge Wells, Kent TN2 3XF
ISBN 978 1 84696 757 3 pbk
Printed in China

We would like to thank: Penny Worms, Shirley Bickler, Suzanne Baker and the National Literacy Trust.

Picture credits (t=top, b=bottom, c=centre, l-left, r=right, OFC= outside front cover)
Corbis: 16-17. Freefoto: OFC, 8. Oshkosh: 12-13. Shutterstock: 9b, 10, 20. Superstock: 5, 6-7, 10-11, 18, 19.
ticktock photography: 4, 14-15. US Coastguard: 17, 21.